© 1999 Havoc Publishing

ISBN 1-57977-157-2

Published by Havoc Publishing
San Diego, California

Artwork © 1999 Kathy Hatch

Please contact us for more information
on Havoc Publishing products.

www.havocpub.com

Havoc Publishing
9808 Waples Street
San Diego, California 92121 U.S.A.

Made in China

THIS RECORD BOOK BELONGS TO:

_____

TEA

LILACS

ROSES

PERENNIALS

great GARDENS

Contents

Contents

My Love of Gardening

I enjoy spending time in my garden because _____

_____

_____

My favorite memories of gardening are _____

_____

_____

_____

_____

_____

"To own a bit of ground, to scratch it with a hoe,
to plant seeds, and watch their renewal of life.-
this is the commonest delight."

Charles Dudley Warner

Mary, Mary quite contrary
how does your garden grow...

DRIED FLOWERS

My Growing Garden

I remember the happiest time I spent gardening was

My Gardening History

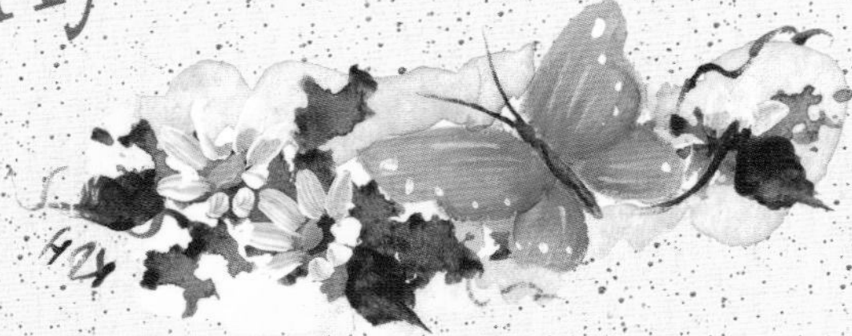

I remember my love of gardening began when I _____

_____

_____

_____

The things I remember most about my first garden _____

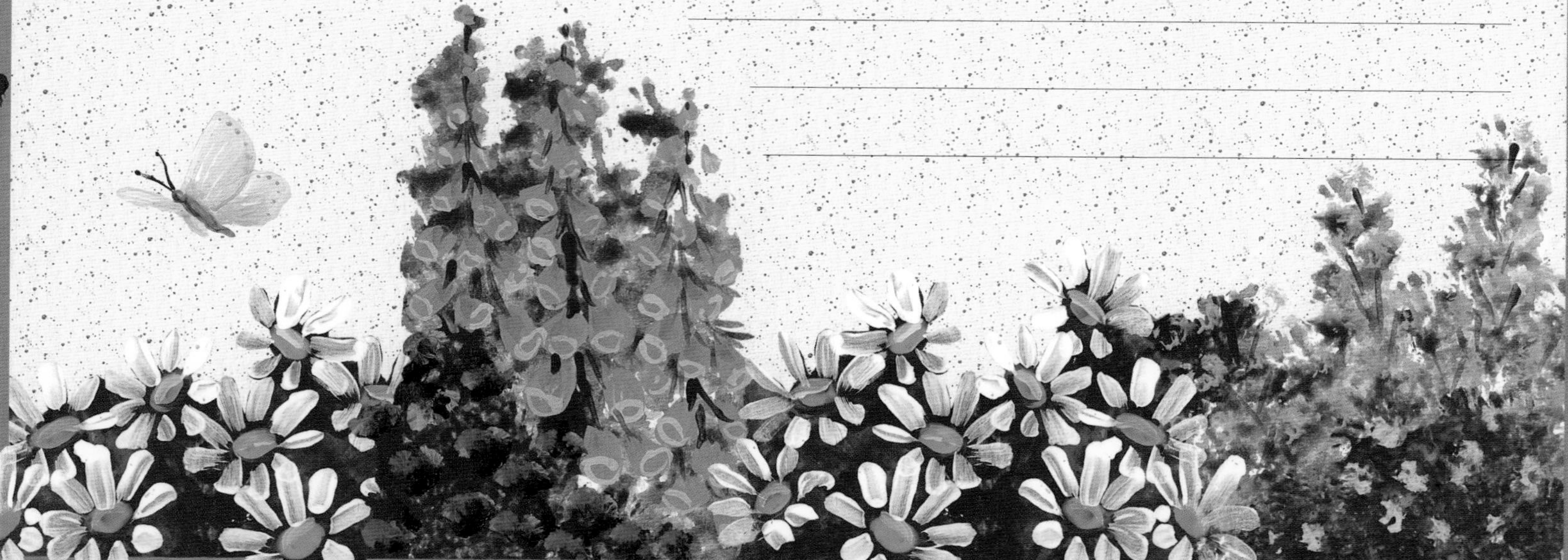

_____

_____

_____

_____

HERB
GARDEN

I recall many successes in gardening. Some of my favorites are

_____

_____

Thinking back, the most ambitious project I have attempted was

_____

_____

_____

_____

All that in this delightful garden grows
Should happy be, and have immortal bliss
Edmund Spenser

DRIED FLOWERS · HERBS · FLOWERS · FLOWERS

My Childhood Days Outdoors

I remember when I was a child I spent time in a special garden that I hold close to my heart. I cherish these special things about that garden

_____

_____

My favorite flowers when I was young were _____

_____

_____

_____

_____

_____

This is the person that inspired my love for gardening _____

_____

_____

_____

_____

Thinking back, this is a gardening project I once helped with _____

_____

_____

_____

_____

_____

_____

_____

Attach Seed Packets Here

SEEDS

Attach Seed Packets Here

SEEDS

My First Garden

I remember as a child I had my first garden here _____

_____

_____

_____

My favorite things about my first garden _____

_____

_____

_____

_____

_____

_____

_____

My first garden that I created was very special to me because

_____

_____

_____

_____

My first garden developed with me. I remember special things I added to help build it from the ground up _____

_____

_____

_____

...with silver bells...

WELCOME

Press Your Favorite Flower Here

Show me your garden
and I shall tell you what you are
Alfred Austin

Learning About Gardening

I have many memories of research that I have done for my garden

_____

_____

_____

_____

I believe some of the most helpful sources I have found are _____

_____

_____

_____

Many times trial and error is the only method for gardening. My fondest memory of a lesson learned is _____

_____

_____

_____

Reflecting back, some of my plants and flowers that have flourished by chance are _____

_____

_____

_____

_____

_____

_____

My Dream Garden

My dreams include a garden filled with many special things

_____

_____

_____

_____

_____

_____

_____

_____

_____

Cut and paste pictures to make your dream garden

Gardens that are Special

A special garden that I like to visit is _____

_____

_____

If I could take one thing from this garden it would be _____

_____

_____

Some of the other gardens that I like to visit are _____

_____

_____

...and cockleshells...

My Special Garden

My garden is very unique in its own way because _____
_____
_____
_____
_____
_____
_____
_____

Photograph

HERB GARDEN

DRIED FLOWERS · HERBS · FLOWERS · FLOWERS · DRIED FLOWERS · HERBS · FLOWERS · HERBS · FLOWERS · DRIED HERBS · HERBS · FLOWERS · FLOWERS · DRIED FLOWERS · HERBS · FLOWERS

Always Making Things Better

Some of the things that I would like to improve in my garden are

_____

_____

_____

_____

_____

_____

_____

_____

_____

Gardens were before gardeners,
but some hours, after the earth

Thomas Browne

My Gardening Goals

Tools of The Trade

I find the essential tools for gardening are _____

_____

_____

I always seem to need a special tool for _____

_____

If I could invent a gardening tool it would be _____

_____

_____

Water is the greatest tool of all

My favorite time to water is this time of day _____

_____

In my garden these plants and flowers require the most water _____

_____

_____

I remember always wanting a birdbath, pond, fountain or the like _____

_____

_____

_____

_____

_____

Photograph

Photograph

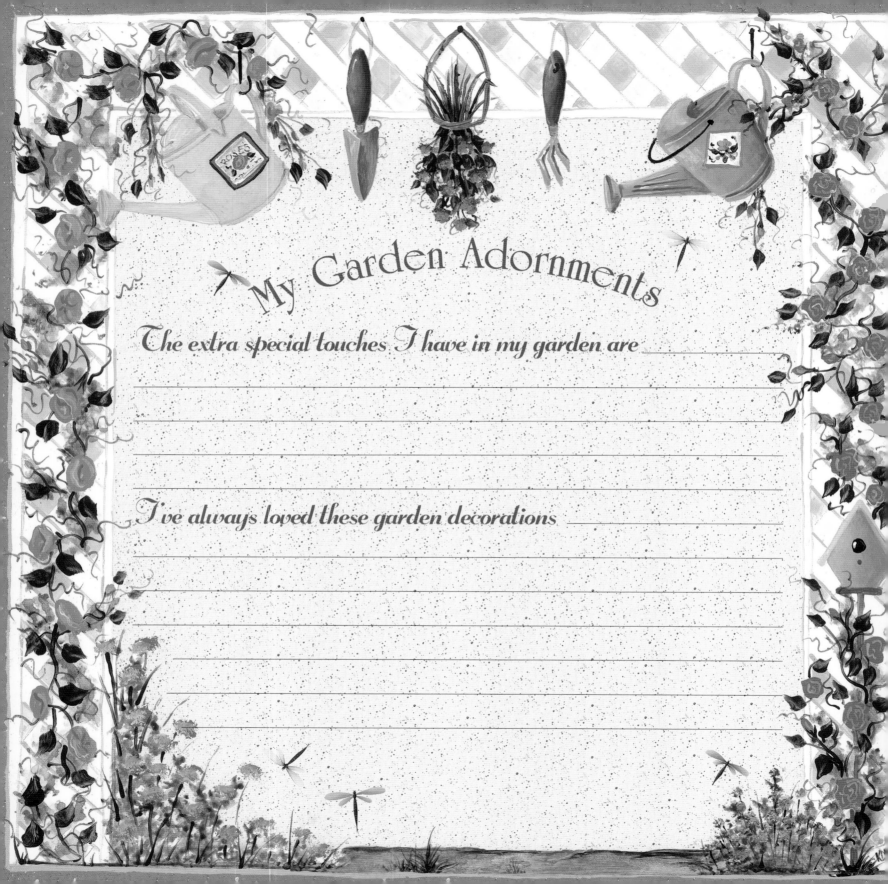

My Garden Adornments

The extra special touches I have in my garden are _____

_____

_____

_____

_____

I've always loved these garden decorations _____

_____

_____

_____

_____

_____

_____

Relaxing in the shade

Shade provides a sense of relaxation in my garden. I have planted my shady areas with _____

_____

_____

Special things I have always wanted to add _____

_____

_____

_____

_____

_____

Photograph

...and pretty maids
all in a row. *Anonymous Nursery Rhyme*

Learning things about gardening

I have received many special tips about gardening. The most helpful tips have been from

_____

_____

_____

_____

_____

_____

_____

Gardening Tips I've picked up

Date: **Season:**   **Tip:**

Press Flowers Here

Press Flowers Here

Watching Flowers Spring Up

SEEDS

My spring garden begins showing growth when _____

_____

_____

Some of my bulbs that come back annually are _____

_____

Some of my favorite spring blooms are _____

_____

_____

_____

_____

_____

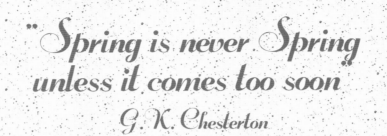

"Spring is never Spring
unless it comes too soon

G. K. Chesterton

Spring Photographs

Spring Photographs

HERB GARDEN

My Garden in the Summer

In my summer garden I like to plant _____

_____

_____

_____

_____

"I should enjoy this summer
flower by flower
as if it were to be
the last summer for me"

Andre Girde

HERB GARDEN

A Plentiful Summer Garden

Some of my favorite fruits and vegetables I like to plant are _____

_____

_____

_____

I remember the most successful fruits and vegetables I have grown were

_____

_____

_____

Just Spending Time Outside

This is the part of gardening that I enjoy most

_____

_____

I remember the most relaxing time in my garden was _____

_____

_____

My favorite place to sit and enjoy my garden is

_____

_____

_____

A Little Free Thinking

Take this book into your garden and write whatever comes to mind

The Feeling of Fall

My garden needs this special attention in the fall _____

_____

_____

_____

Some things I tend to do are _____

_____

_____

I remember my favorite fall gardening was spent _____

_____

_____

_____

_____

Preparing my garden for the coming winter involves _____

_____

_____

_____

_____

_____

My favorite fall leaves are these _____

_____

_____

_____

_____

_____

My Garden in the Wintertime

My garden still has growth in the winter. These special plants are

_____

_____

_____

_____

I remember every year to take these special precautions for winter

_____

_____

_____

_____

My Favorite Winter Photograph

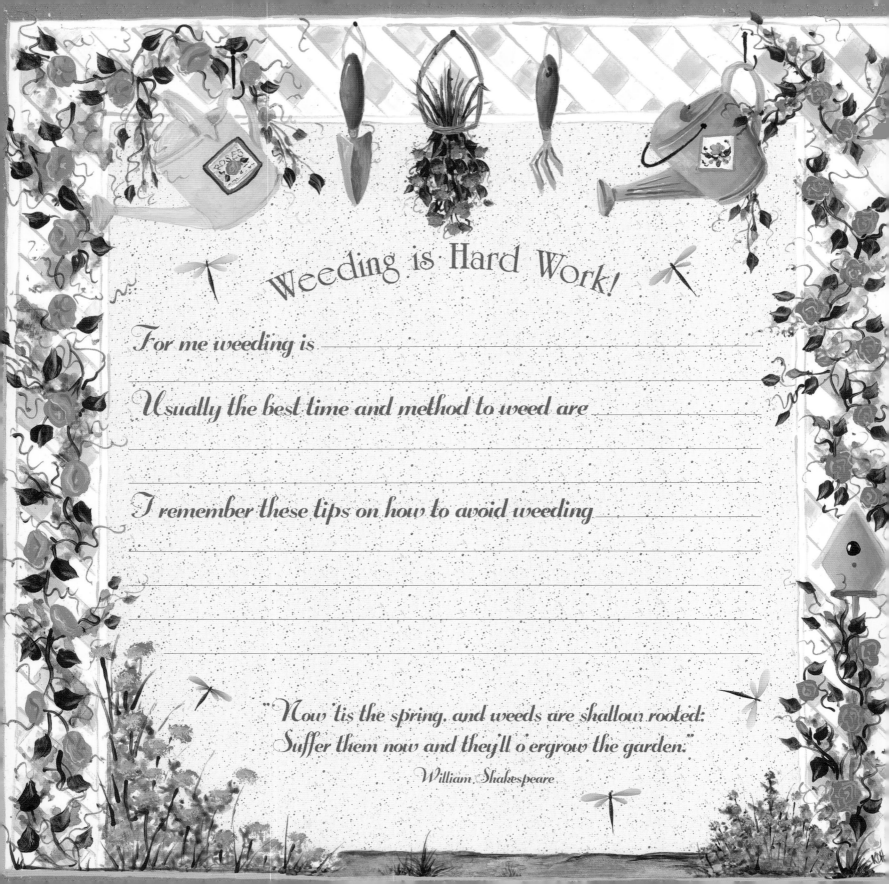

Weeding is Hard Work!

For me weeding is _____

_____

Usually the best time and method to weed are _____

_____

_____

I remember these tips on how to avoid weeding _____

_____

_____

_____

"Now 'tis the spring, and weeds are shallow rooted:
Suffer them now and they'll o'ergrow the garden."
William Shakespeare

Before & After
Weeding Photographs

Amazing Annuals

My favorite annuals are _____

_____

_____

In the past, I have made flower arrangements and bouquets from these annuals _____

_____

_____

_____

_____

_____

Perfect Perennials

My favorite perennials are _____

_____

_____

_____

_____

_____ told me the best time to plant perennials is

_____

_____

*"Perennials, pleasures, plants
and wholesome harvest reaps."*
Amos Bronson Alcott

"I know a little garden close,
set thick with lily and red rose,
Where I might wander if I might
From dewy morn to dewy night."

William Morris

Nature's Visitors

Nature's creatures add an extra special element to my garden. To make little visitors feel welcome I have added these feeders and houses to my garden

_____

_____

_____

I remember when _____ *gave me tips on what to do for unwelcome visitors* _____

_____

_____

HERB
GARDEN

My favorite garden visitor has always been _____
because _____
_____
_____
_____
_____
_____
_____

Special Notes & Thoughts

Available Record Books from Havoc

A Celebration of Memories
A Circle of Love
Baby
College Life
Couples
Family

Forever Friends
Friendship
Generations
Girlfriends
Grandmother
Grandparents

Heart to Heart
It's All About Me!
Memories of My Garden
Mom
Mothers & Daughters
Mother & Son
My Pregnancy

Our Honeymoon
Our Wedding
School Days
Sisters
Tying the Knot
Twins
Your First Five Years

www.havocpub.com